ATTACK of the HANGRIES

HUNGRY + ANGRY = HANGRY

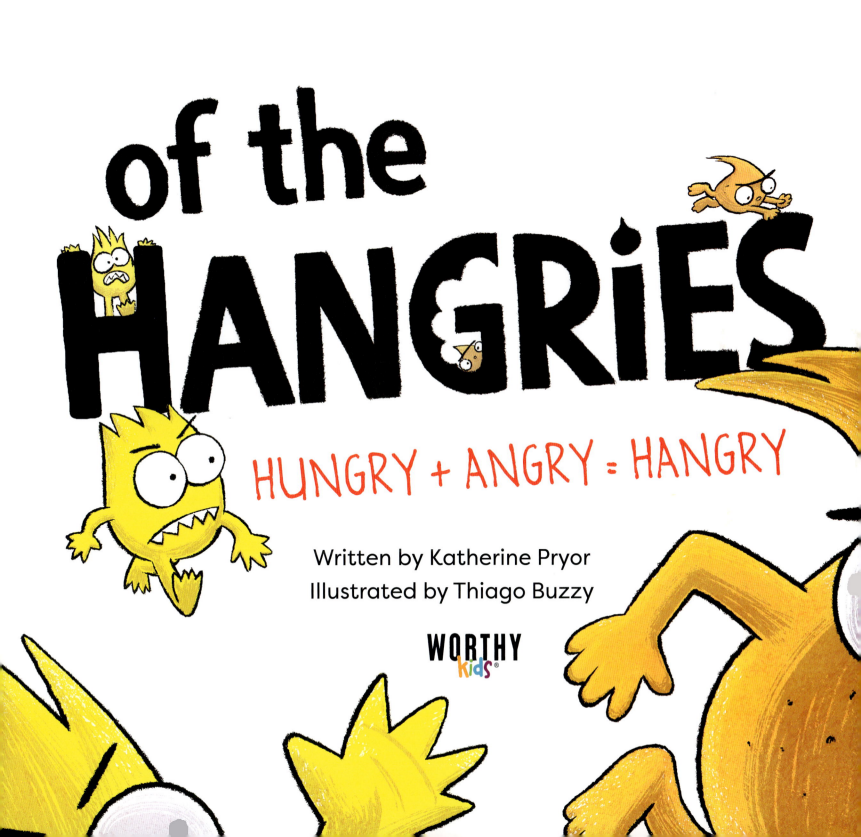

of the HANGRIES

HUNGRY + ANGRY = HANGRY

Written by Katherine Pryor
Illustrated by Thiago Buzzy

WORTHY kids

spelunking in the caves of Quintana Roo.

You might be having a **terrible** day.

You might be having a **fantastic** day.

ATTACK!
THE **HANGRIES** TAKE OVER!

Your brain scrambles.
Your limbs flail.
All you want to do is SCREAM!
AT EVERYONE! FOR ANYTHING!

You look around.
Somehow, the room
is destroyed.

Maybe you're sitting in math class, **when suddenly...**

ATTACK!

You flip out over a tricky problem and tear your homework to shreds.

As you chew the chunk of cheese that found its way into your mouth, you wonder:

Why did that happen?

What are the **Hangries**?

Where do they come from?

Did they **leap** out from behind the twisty slide?

Did they **pounce** on your shoulders and make you throw that ball at Coach Thompson's tush?

Did they jump down your throat and bounce on your tongue, and THAT'S why you yelled the number one bad word on your do-not-say list?

Nope.

If that's not what happened, then what?

Uh-oh!

That's when the Hangries attack.

But why? Food gives our bodies energy.

When we don't eat, our bodies are missing the fuel they need to think and run and explore.

If your fuel level gets too low, your body sends little messengers called **hormones** through your blood to let you know there's a problem.

Hormones are chemicals that travel between different parts of your body to tell it what to do.

The hormones that tell us when we have gone too long without food are called **adrenaline** and **cortisol**.

They're sending an emergency signal to your brain saying,

"HELP!" "FUEL LOW!"

"Mortal peril!!" "Impending starvation!"

"FEED ME!!!"

Adrenaline

is a hormone our body produces to help us through scary or dangerous situations.

It can provide temporary speed or strength and is known for fueling our "fight-or-flight" response to danger.

Great for running away from lions. Not so great for math class.

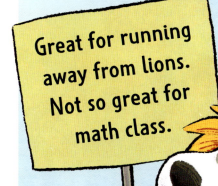

Cortisol

is a hormone our bodies produce to help us respond to stress.

Cortisol has a lot of important jobs. One of them is to release a type of sugar to give you fast energy when your body feels stressed.

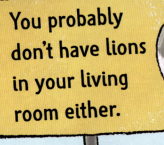

You probably don't have lions in your living room either.

The Hangries are really just your friendly hormones **adrenaline** and **cortisol** trying to help.

But when we don't listen, those little helpers

can become little **monsters**.

So, how can you keep the Hangries away?

Everyone needs to eat several times a day to keep their fuel levels up.

It may seem like you just ate a little bit ago, but it takes a lot of energy to grow and play and run like you do.

So, if you feel your fuel gauge getting low . . .

More to Know...

Foods to Banish the Hangries

Remember, hungry is the first part of hangry:

HUNGRY + ANGRY = HANGRY

How do you keep the Hangries from taking over? It starts with *what* you eat. To keep the Hangries away, you want to eat foods that take time to digest.

What foods take longer to digest? **Whole grains**, like wheat bread, brown rice, and oatmeal are good choices. Most **vegetables** and **fruits** are good choices too. Or you can look for **proteins** like eggs, nuts, fish, or meat.

But how can all these foods be good for keeping the Hangries away when they're so different? They're all loaded with fiber or protein that will allow them to hang out in your digestive system a while, so you feel full longer! The fats that some of these foods contain provide a backup source of energy with a slow release.

A balanced meal will include a blend of proteins, fruits or veggies, and grains. A Hangry-fighting lunch might be a turkey sandwich on whole-grain bread with carrots and strawberries on the side. Breakfast might be oatmeal with fruit and nuts or a burrito with beans and veggies. There are so many combinations to choose from!

When you eat is important too. Try not to skip meals. Food gives your body energy, and your body needs energy all day long.

Fuel Up Between Meals

What about between meals, when that soccer game or music lesson leaves you feeling hungry? You want to reach for foods with fiber, protein, and fats here too. **Some good choices are:**

Apple or carrot sticks with peanut butter

Smashed avocado on toast

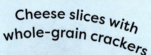

Cheese slices with whole-grain crackers

Trail mix

Veggies with hummus

Beware! Maybe you're thinking, *I'd rather have a donut (isn't that like bread?) or some potato chips (aren't potatoes vegetables?).*

Reaching for something like candy or chips or cookies might seem like a simple fix, but your body digests them really quickly. They will give you a quick burst of energy but then leave you dragging.

What Happens to Your Food After You Eat?
Food takes a pretty impressive journey through your body!

- First you chew and swallow your food—that part you already know.

- Then the chewed food is squeezed down your **esophagus** by wavelike muscle contractions that move it into your stomach.

- With the help of digestive juices, your **stomach** muscle churns the food into smaller, liquid-y pieces that travel to your small intestine.

- The **small intestine** absorbs as many nutrients from the food as possible before contractions push what remains into your large intestine.

- Then your **large intestine** absorbs any last nutrients, minerals, and water from what's left. What can't be absorbed or isn't useful to your body rides a twisty intestinal roller coaster toward a stinky grand finale—the toilet.

The Vagus Nerve

The vagus nerve travels from your brain to your lower intestine and is a bit like your body's superhighway. Information zooms between your brain and internal organs. When your stomach is empty, it sends a message to your brain saying, **"Hey, I'm hungry."**

When your brain senses food is on the way, it sends signals along the vagus nerve to tell the stomach to start producing hormones that will help you to digest it.

What's That Noise?

That hungry rumbling is the sound of your stomach muscles contracting as they get ready for food. The sound is loudest when your stomach is empty.

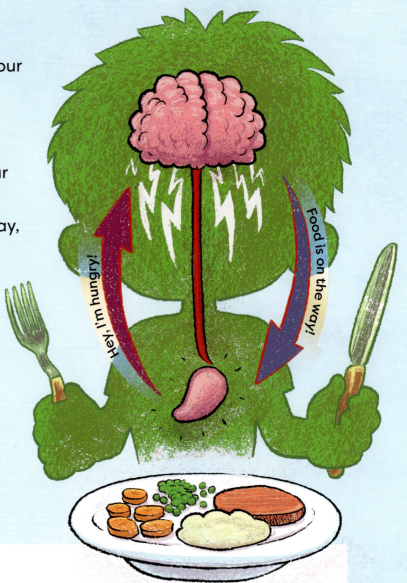

Fun Facts

- Humans can make 4 to 6 cups of saliva each day.
- A human small intestine can be 18 to 22 feet long—that's longer than the average car!
- Trillions of bacteria live in your large intestine to help you digest your food.
- The masseter (jaw-to-cheek muscle) is one of the strongest muscles in our bodies.

For Maryann van Drielen, aka Mom, champion banisher of the Hangries. –K.P.

For Camila, my wife, who always knows when I need a snack, or encouragement. –T.B.

With gratitude to Erin MacDougall, PhD, and Cynthia Lair, author and educator, for helping us understand how food fuels the body.

ISBN: 978-1-5460-0812-5 | WorthyKids, Hachette Book Group, 1290 Avenue of the Americas, New York, NY 10104 | Text copyright © 2025 by Katherine Pryor | Art copyright © 2025 by Thiago Buzzy | Distributed in the United Kingdom by Hachette UK Ltd., Carmelite House, 50 Victoria Embankment, London, EC4Y 0DZ | Distributed in Europe by Hachette Livre, 58 rue Jean Bluezen, 92 178 Vanves Cedex, France | All rights reserved. No part of this publication may be reproduced or transmitted in any form or by any means, electronic or mechanical, including photocopy, recording, or any information storage and retrieval system, without permission in writing from the publisher. | WorthyKids is a registered trademark of Hachette Book Group, Inc.
LCCN: 2025003802

Designed by Eve DeGrie
Printed and bound in Dongguan, China | APS • 06/25
2 4 6 8 10 9 7 5 3 1